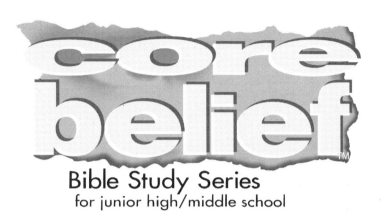

core belief™

Bible Study Series
for junior high/middle school

THE TRUTH ABOUT THE
Spiritual Realm

Group
Loveland, Colorado

The Truth About the Spiritual Realm

Core Belief Bible Study Series

Copyright © 1997 Group Publishing, Inc.

Credits

Editor: Karl Leuthauser
Creative Development Editor: Paul Woods
Chief Creative Officer: Joani Schultz
Copy Editors: Dena Twinem and Pamela Shoup
Art Director: Bill Fisher
Computer Graphic Artist: Ray Tollison
Photographer: Craig DeMartino
Production Manager: Gingar Kunkel

ISBN 0-7644-0857-7
10 9 8 7 6 5 4 3 2 1   06 05 04 03 02 01 00 99 98 97

Printed in the United States of America.

Bible Study Series
for junior high/middle school

contents:

the Core Belief: ▼The Spiritual Realm

Today's young people trust what their five senses tell them. They believe in what they can see, hear, smell, touch, and taste. Yet they have a spiritual hunger for something that goes beyond what they can sense.

It's there—an entire spiritual realm waging battles that many fail to perceive. God's spiritual dominion battles Satan's on a daily basis.

Fortunately, we already know that God has won and will continue to win the war. Because of God's victory, we have the tools and strength necessary to be victorious in our daily struggle against "every proud thing that raises itself against the knowledge of God (2 Corinthians 10:5)."

the ▼Helpful Stuff

^{the} ▼Studies

The Spiritual Realm as a Core Christian Belief

Although we can't touch or see the spiritual realm, it's as real as the rest of our world. According to the Bible, spirits—both good and evil—exist around us. A battle rages between the spiritual followers of Satan and the followers of God. Angels and demons seek to influence the things we do—either by protecting us or by trying to lead us to destruction. In the end, we know that God will win the war, but in the meantime, multitudes of people are being deceived by our adversary, the devil.

Your young people see all sorts of distorted images of the spiritual world. They hear bits and pieces of all kinds of philosophies from all different directions. And they may not know what to believe. Use the studies within this Core Christian Belief to help your kids better understand what the spirit world is all about.

In the first study of this book, kids will have an opportunity to learn about **spiritual warfare.** Your kids may be aware that there is a battle going on, but they may be confused about who the warriors are and where the battleground is. This study will help kids understand the role that their own choices, God, angels, and demons play in the spiritual battle.

In the second study, kids will be encouraged to take an honest look at **music.** They can discover that music has an effect on how we feel, what we do, and even who we are. Kids will be challenged with the fact that music can have spiritual implications since we are spiritual as well as physical beings.

In the third study, kids can begin an honest dialogue about drug **abuse.** By discussing the damage and pain that drugs often lead to, kids can discover that not everything spiritual is good.

The final study deals with one of the most exciting aspects of Christian spirituality. Kids will be reminded that **heaven** is real and that the choices they make now have eternal significance. They'll be encouraged to leave behind that which is unimportant as they press on toward their eternal reward.

*For a more comprehensive look at this Core Christian Belief, read Group's **Get Real: Making Core Christian Beliefs Relevant to Teenagers.***

DEPTHFINDER

HOW THE BIBLE DESCRIBES THE SPIRITUAL REALM

To help you effectively guide your kids toward this Core Christian Belief, use these overviews as a launching point for a more in-depth study of the spiritual realm:

The Bible tells of two radically different spiritual kingdoms: the dominion ruled by God and the dominion ruled by Satan. The two are constantly in conflict, but God will eventually completely destroy Satan's dominion (Psalm 148:2-5; Colossians 2:15; Hebrews 2:14; 1 John 3:8; Jude 6; and Revelation 5:11; 20:7-10).

● **God's spiritual dominion includes:**

God—God isn't a being made up of matter as we are but is a "spirit" being. Scripture passages that give God arms, hands, eyes, and the like are simply human attempts to describe God's actions in terms we understand. God exists in three persons: Father, Jesus, and Holy Spirit. Jesus became human—without losing his divinity—to dwell on earth and die as a sacrifice for human sin (Luke 24:39; John 4:24; 10:25-30; 14:26; 15:26; Romans 1:20; and Colossians 1:15).

Angels—God created all angels. They're sentient, individual spiritual beings with limited superhuman abilities. Angels are not people who have died and gone to heaven, as some myths tend to suggest. The Bible indicates the existence of millions of angels, organized into various divisions and fulfilling various roles. Angels worship God in heaven and seek to work out his will on earth by guiding people and nations, protecting churches and people, and punishing those who oppose God (2 Samuel 14:20; Daniel 6:22; 10:4-21; Matthew 18:10; 26:53; Luke 20:36; Acts 12:21-23; Colossians 1:16; 2 Peter 2:11; and Revelation 5:11).

Christians—Humans are spiritual beings, though we exist in material bodies. Those who have a faith relationship with God through Jesus' death and resurrection have experienced spiritual regeneration. When our bodies die, we don't become angels or come back as other beings; instead, we go to live with Christ as spirits. At the final resurrection, our spirits will receive new spiritual bodies (Genesis 2:7; Job 32:8; Ecclesiastes 12:7; 2 Corinthians 5:1-8; and James 2:26).

Heaven—Heaven can be defined simply as God's ultimate dwelling place. Jesus referred to it as "my Father's house." It's a place where God's people will rest, worship, and live in harmony and fellowship with one another. There will be no death, no pain, and no sorrow. We'll receive rewards based on how we served God during our time on earth. Our minds can't imagine how wonderful it will be to spend eternity in heaven with God (John 14:2-3; Hebrews 4:9-11; James 1:12; and Revelation 19:1; 21:3-4).

● **Satan's spiritual dominion includes:**

Satan—God created Satan as a holy angel. However, Satan chose to reject God and set himself up against God. Satan is a real being and has great power, but he is neither all-powerful nor all-knowing as God is. Satan rules the forces of evil in our world, directing demonic spirits against God and people. He uses and sometimes possesses people in his attempts to disrupt God's working. He deceives, accuses, tempts, and slanders people, seeking to draw them away from God. God will eventually send Satan and all who follow him into eternal punishment (John 8:44; 14:30; 16:11; Ephesians 2:2; Colossians 1:16; 1 Thessalonians 2:18; 1 Peter 5:8; 1 John 3:8; and Revelation 20:7-10).

Demons—Demons are angels, created by God, who followed Satan and his dominion of evil instead of being true to God. Demonic spirits are dedicated to opposing God and defeating his will. They're involved in tempting people to do wrong, and they can take control of individuals to advance Satan's cause. Demons seek to deceive people, directing them to walk—sometimes unknowingly—down Satan's path. At the final judgment, demons will be judged with Satan (Matthew 25:41; Mark 5:2-9; Luke 13:10-16; John 13:27; Acts 10:38; and Ephesians 2:2).

Non-Christians—These spirits of humans don't have a faith relationship with God through Jesus' death and resurrection, and they face immediate imprisonment at the death of the body. They'll endure torment from that moment on. They don't become demons, nor are they reincarnated to live on earth again as animals or people.

In the end they'll be cast into the lake of fire with Satan and all who follow him (Luke 16:23, 26; 1 Peter 2:9; 3:19; Hebrews 9:27; and Revelation 20:7-15; 22:11-15).

Hell—Hell is the final destination of Satan and all who reject faith in Jesus. It can be defined simply as a place totally separated from God. The Bible describes it as a place of continuous, everlasting fire—a place of eternal torment. Adding to the torment will be the realization that believing in Jesus would have led to eternity with God instead of eternal punishment (Matthew 8:12; 25:41; Mark 9:43; Luke 12:47-48; 1 Corinthians 3:15; and Revelation 14:10-11; 20:13-15).

● **People on earth are involved in the constant battle between opposing spiritual dominions.** We're in the midst of a spiritual battle—the forces of God and good against the forces of Satan and evil. That doesn't mean that those who don't believe as we do are our enemies; instead, our enemies are Satan and the demonic spirits who seek to deceive and destroy us. We're instructed to guard and arm ourselves against the enemies, to support and encourage each other, and to enlist all we can to join us in the battle (Job 1:6–2:7; Daniel 10:12-13; Zechariah 3:1-2; Matthew 5:43-46; 28:18-20; Ephesians 6:10-18; James 4:7; 1 Peter 5:8; and Jude 9).

Understanding all the Bible says about the spiritual realm is difficult. Few of us will ever grasp it completely. But fortunately for us, the Bible makes the important parts clear. When your kids understand that God and his angels are waiting to help them withstand Satan's onslaught, they'll be better prepared to face our spiritual world with a confident faith.

CORE CHRISTIAN BELIEF OVERVIEW

Here are the twenty-four Core Christian Belief categories that form the backbone of Core Belief Bible Study Series:

The Nature of God	Jesus Christ	The Holy Spirit
Humanity	Evil	Suffering
Creation	The Spiritual Realm	The Bible
Salvation	Spiritual Growth	Personal Character
God's Justice	Sin & Forgiveness	The Last Days
Love	The Church	Worship
Authority	Prayer	Family
Service	Relationships	Sharing Faith

Look for Group's Core Belief Bible Study Series books in these other Core Christian Beliefs!

about

Bible Study Series
for junior high/middle school

Think for a moment about your young people. When your students walk out of your youth program after they graduate from junior high or high school, what do you want them to know? What foundation do you want them to have so they can make wise choices?

You probably want them to know the essentials of the Christian faith. You want them to base everything they do on the foundational truths of Christianity. Are you meeting this goal?

If you have any doubt that your kids will walk into adulthood knowing and living by the tenets of the Christian faith, then you've picked up the right book. All the books in Group's Core Belief Bible Study Series encourage young people to discover the essentials of Christianity and to put those essentials into practice. Let us explain...

What Is Group's Core Belief Bible Study Series?

Group's Core Belief Bible Study Series is a biblically in-depth study series for junior high and senior high teenagers. This Bible study series utilizes four defining commitments to create each study. These "plumb lines" provide structure and continuity for every activity, study, project, and discussion. They are:

● **A Commitment to Biblical Depth**—Core Belief Bible Study Series is founded on the belief that kids not only *can* understand the deeper truths of the Bible but also *want* to understand them. Therefore, the activities and studies in this series strive to explain the "why" behind every truth we explore. That way, kids learn principles, not just rules.

● **A Commitment to Relevance**—Most kids aren't interested in abstract theories or doctrines about the universe. They want to know how to live successfully right now, today, in the heat of problems they can't ignore. Because of this, each study connects a real-life need with biblical principles that speak directly to that need. This study series finally bridges the gap between Bible truths and the real-world issues kids face.

● **A Commitment to Variety**—Today's young people have been raised in a sound bite world. They demand variety. For that reason, no two meetings in this study series are shaped exactly the same.

● **A Commitment to Active and Interactive Learning**—Active learning is learning by doing. Interactive learning simply takes active learning a step further by having kids teach each other what they've learned. It's a process that helps kids internalize and remember their discoveries.

For a more detailed description of these concepts, see the section titled "Why Active and Interactive Learning Works With Teenagers" beginning on page 57.

So how can you accomplish all this in a set of four easy-to-lead Bible studies? By weaving together various "power" elements to produce a fun experience that leaves kids challenged and encouraged.

Turn the page to take a look at some of the power elements used in this series.

THE ISSUE: Relationships

Betrayed!

HELPING KIDS DEAL WITH REJECTION FROM THE PEOPLE THEY LOVE

by Jennifer Carrell

THE POINT:

God is love.

■ Betrayal has very little shock value for this generation. It's as commonplace as compact discs and mosh pits. For many kids today, betrayal characterizes their parents' wedding vows. It's part of their curriculum at school; it defines the headlines and evening news. Betrayal is not only accepted—it's expected. ■ At the heart of such acceptance lies the belief that nothing is absolute. No vow, no law, no promise can be trusted. Relationships are betrayed at the earliest convenience. Repeatedly, kids see that something called "love" lasts just as long as it's _____ permanence. But deep inside, they hunger to see a

The Study
AT A GLANCE

SECTION	MINUTES	WHAT STUDENTS WILL DO	SUPPLIES
Discussion Starter	up to 5	JUMP-START—Identify some of the most common themes in today's movies.	Newsprint, marker
Investigation of Betrayal	12 to 15	REALITY CHECK—Form groups to compare anonymous, real-life stories of betrayal with experiences in their own lives.	"Profiles of Betrayal" handouts (p. 20), highlighter pens, newsprint, marker, tape
	3 to 5	WHO BETRAYED WHOM?—Guess the identities of the people profiled in the handouts.	Paper, tape, pen
Investigation of True Love	15 to 18	SOURCE WORK—Study and discuss God's definition of perfect love.	Bibles, newsprint, marker
	5 to 7	LOVE MESSAGES—Create unique ways to send a "message of love" to the victims of betrayal they've been studying.	Newsprint, markers, tape
Personal Application	10 to 15	SYMBOLIC LOVE—Give a partner a personal symbol of perfect love.	Paper lunch sack, pens, scissors, paper, catalogs

notes:

● **A Relevant Topic**—More than ever before, kids live in the now. What matters to them and what attracts their hearts is what's happening in their world at this moment. For this reason, every Core Belief Bible Study focuses on a particular hot topic that kids care about.

● **A Core Christian Belief**—Group's Core Belief Bible Study Series organizes the wealth of Christian truth and experience into twenty-four Core Christian Belief categories. These twenty-four headings act as umbrellas for a collection of detailed beliefs that define Christianity and set it apart from the world and every other religion. Each book in this series features one Core Christian Belief with lessons suited for junior high or senior high students.

"But," you ask, "won't my kids be bored talking about all these spiritual beliefs?" No way! As a youth leader, you know the value of using hot topics to connect with young people. Ultimately teenagers talk about issues because they're searching for meaning in their lives. They want to find the one equation that will make sense of all the confusing events happening around them. Each Core Belief Bible Study answers that need by connecting a hot topic with a powerful Christian principle. Kids walk away from the study with something more solid than just the shifting ebb and flow of their own opinions. They walk away with a deeper understanding of their Christian faith.

● **The Point**—This simple statement is designed to be the intersection between the Core Christian Belief and the hot topic. Everything in the study ultimately focuses on The Point so that kids study it and allow it time to sink into their hearts.

● **The Study at a Glance**—A quick look at this chart will tell you what kids will do, how long it will take them to do it, and what supplies you'll need to get it done.

The Bibliography Connection entries

THE POINT OF BETRAYED!:

God is love.

THE BIBLE CONNECTION

1 JOHN 4:7-21   The Apostle John explains the nature and definition of perfect love.

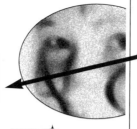

In this study, kids will compare the imperfect love defined in real-life stories of betrayal to God's definition of perfect love.

By making this comparison, kids can discover that God is love and therefore incapable of betraying them. Then they'll be able to recognize the incredible opportunity God of...
relationship worthy of their absolute trust.

Explore the verses in The Bible Connection...
mation in the Depthfinder boxes throughout...
understanding of how these Scriptures conne...

LEADER TIP

THE STUDY

DISCUSSION STARTER ▼

Jump-Start (up to 5 minutes) As kids arrive, ask them to think...
common themes in movies, books, TV show...
have kids each contribute ideas for a mast...
two other kids in the room and sharing...
sider providing copies of People maga...
what's currently showing on television or at th...
their suggestions, write their respon...s on new
come up with a lot of great idea. Even tho...
ent, look through this list and...ry to discov...
ments most of these themes...ave in comm...

After kids make several su...gestions, mention...
responses are connected wi...h the idea of betra...

● **Why do you think...**etrayal is such a co...

Betrayed! 17

The Bible Connection—This is the power base of each study. Whether it's just one verse or several chapters, The Bible Connection provides the vital link between kids' minds and their hearts. The content of each Core Belief Bible Study reflects the belief that the true power of God—the power to expose, heal, and change kids' lives—is contained in his Word.

LEADER TIP for The Study

Because this topic can be so powerful and relevant to kids' lives, your group members may be tempted to get caught up in issues and lose sight of the deeper biblical principle found in The Point. Help your kids grasp The Point by guiding kids to focus on the biblical investigation and discussing how God's truth connects with reality in their lives.

DEPTHFINDER   UNDERSTANDING INTEGRITY

Your students may not be entirely familiar with the meaning of integrity, especially as it might apply to God's character in the Trinity. Use these definitions (taken from Webster's II New Riverside Dictionary) and other information to help you guide kids toward a better understanding of how God maintains integrity through the three expressions of the Trinity.

Integrity: 1. Firm adherence to a code or standard of values. 2. The state of being unimpaired. 3. The quality or condition of being undivided.

Synonyms for integrity include probity, completeness, wholeness, soundness, and perfection.

Our word "integrity" comes from the Latin word *integritas*, which means soundness. *Integritas* is also the root of the word "integer," which means "whole or complete," as in a "whole" number.

The Hebrew word that's often translated "integrity" (for example, in Psalm 25:21 [NIV]) is *tam*. It means whole, perfect, sincere, and honest.

CREATIVE GOD-EXPLORATION ▼

Top Hats (18 to 20 minutes) Form three groups, with each trio member from the previous activity going to a different group. Give each group Bibles, paper, and pens, and assign each group a different hat God wears: Father, Son, or Holy Spirit.
...s their goal is to write one list describing what God does in the...God's character.

Depthfinder Boxes—These informative sidelights located throughout each study add insight into a particular passage, word, historical fact, or Christian doctrine. Depthfinder boxes also provide insight into teen culture, adolescent development, current events, and philosophy.

Holy Profiles

Your assigned Bible passage describes how a particular person or group responded when confronted with God's holiness. Use the information in your passage to help your group discuss the questions below. Then use your flashlights to teach the other two groups what you discover.

■ Based on your passage, what does holiness look like?

■ What does holiness sound like?

■ When people see God's holiness, how does it affect them?

■ How is this response to God's holiness like humility?

■ Based on your passage, how would you describe humility?

■ Why is humility an appropriate human response to God's holiness?

■ Based on what you see in your passage, do you think you are a humble person? Why or why not?

■ What's one way you could develop humility in your life this week?

● **Leader Tips**—These handy information boxes coach you through the study, offering helpful suggestions on everything from altering activities for different-sized groups to streamlining discussions to using effective discipline techniques.

● **Handouts**—Most Core Belief Bible Studies include photocopiable handouts to use with your group. Handouts might take the form of a fun game, a lively discussion starter, or a challenging study page for kids to take home—anything to make your study more meaningful and effective.

The Last Word on Core Belief Bible Studies

Soon after you begin to use Group's Core Belief Bible Study Series, you'll see signs of real growth in your group members. Your kids will gain a deeper understanding of the Bible and of their own Christian faith. They'll see more clearly how a relationship with Jesus affects their daily lives. And they'll grow closer to God.

But that's not all. You'll also see kids grow closer to one another.

That's because this series is founded on the principle that Christian faith grows best in the context of relationship. Each study uses a variety of interactive pairs and small groups and always includes discussion questions that promote deeper relationships. The friendships kids will build through this study series will enable them to grow *together* toward a deeper relationship with God.

The Unseen War

war

by Lisa Hitaffer

THE POINT:

Angels and demons are active in your life.

■ According to an article in Time magazine, sixty-nine percent of Americans believe angels exist. But what do they believe about angels? Many followers of the New Age movement claim that they have personal angelic spirit-guides who help and protect them. Some people believe that we all become angels after we die. Others say angels are dear family members who have returned from the dead to help them through a difficult time in life. ■ There seems to be just as much confusion about demons. Many deny the existence of demons altogether. Some believe demons offer opportunity for power and gain. Some hold to the medieval tradition that demons are jolly tricksters dressed in red suits. ■ According to the Bible, angels and demons are real. They have real power that is limited by God's authority. The Bible explains that we are in a spiritual battle where angels, demons, and humans all play an important role. Teenagers need a biblical understanding of the influence these forces can have on their lives, and they need to understand their own role in the spiritual battle. Use this study to help your kids find the biblical truth about angels, demons, and the war they are in.

The Study
AT A GLANCE

the study at a glance

SECTION	MINUTES	WHAT STUDENTS WILL DO	SUPPLIES
Opening Game	10 to 15	WAR GAMES—Play a game that simulates what spiritual warfare might be like.	Bible, masking tape, paper, marker, blindfolds
Bible Exploration	5 to 10	PLAYING WITH POWER—Investigate what Scripture says about humans, angels, and demons.	Bibles, pencils, paper, "Playing With Power" handouts (p. 22)
	15 to 20	HEAVENLY STORIES—Re-create stories to demonstrate what roles angels and demons may play.	Bibles, "Unseen Messengers" handouts (pp. 23-24), "Playing With Power" handouts from last activity, pencils, paper
Personal Application	10 to 15	ARMOR ALL—Find practical uses for the armor of God, and pray with each other.	Bibles, paper, pencils

notes:

THE POINT OF *THE UNSEEN WAR:*

Angels and demons are active in your life.

THE BIBLE CONNECTION

GENESIS 19:1-22; EXODUS 23:20-23; LUKE 22:39-43; HEBREWS 1:5-7,14	These passages describe the activity of angels.
MATTHEW 8:28-32; 16:21-23; 1 PETER 5:8-9; REVELATION 12:7-12	These passages describe the activity of demons.
LUKE 10:17-20; ACTS 16:16-18; 2 CORINTHIANS 10:3-6; EPHESIANS 6:10-18	These passages describe the role humans have in spiritual warfare.
2 CORINTHIANS 11:13-15	This passage explains that Satan and his followers often pretend to do what's right.
PHILIPPIANS 2:9-11	This passage explains that everyone and everything is subject to Christ Jesus.

LEADER TIP for The Study

Because this topic can be so powerful and relevant to kids' lives, your group members may be tempted to get caught up in issues and lose sight of the deeper biblical principle found in The Point. Help your kids grasp The Point by guiding kids to focus on the biblical investigation and discussing how God's truth connects with reality in their lives.

I n this study, students will play a game that simulates possible aspects of spiritual warfare; search Scripture for a balanced understanding of angels, demons, and humans; re-create stories to demonstrate spiritual activity; and brainstorm practical applications for the armor of God.

By doing this, students can learn that neither angels, demons, nor humans are beyond God's power. They can see that God hasn't left us without defenses and that God sends angels for our benefit and his glory.

BEFORE THE STUDY

For the "War Games" activity, use masking tape to outline two goal areas that are each large enough for one-third of your class to stand in. Put the goals as far apart from each other as your meeting room allows. Use a marker to write "Safety" on a sheet of paper, and tape the sheet on a wall near one of the goals. Write "Death" on another sheet of paper, and tape that sheet on a wall near the other goal.

For the "Armor All" activity, write each of the following phrases on separate slips of paper: "belt of truth," "breastplate of righteousness," "feet ready with the gospel of peace," "shield of faith," "helmet of salvation," "sword of the Spirit which is the Word of God," and "prayer."

THE STUDY

OPENING GAME ▼

LEADER TIP
for War Games

If your meeting area has a bright light or a consistent sound that would help blindfolded students find their way to the goal areas without guidance, wait until they're blindfolded to hang up the "Safety" and "Death" signs.

LEADER TIP
for The Study

Whenever groups discuss a list of questions, write the questions on newsprint and tape the newsprint to the wall so groups can discuss the questions at their own pace.

War Games (10 to 15 minutes)

As kids arrive, give one-third of them blindfolds and ask them to put the blindfolds on. Give one-half of the students without blindfolds a sheet of paper. Say: **Those of you with blindfolds will act as humans, those of you with a sheet of paper will act as angels, and those of you with neither blindfolds nor paper are going to act as demons. The angels' goal is to guide the humans to step into the area labeled "Safety." The demons' goal is to encourage the humans to step into the area labeled "Death." The humans' goal is to make it to the safety area and avoid the death area. Once a human steps into an area, the angel or demon must tell him or her to freeze and the human may not move. The demons and angels cannot touch the humans. The angels can try to encourage or convince the humans to go to the safety area, but they can't lie to the humans. The demons can trick or lie to the humans to get them to go to the death area. Are there any questions?**

Instruct the students acting as demons to go up to the humans, put their hands on the humans' shoulders, and spin the humans around five times. Read 2 Corinthians 11:13-15 aloud to the group. Remind kids that the demons' most effective tactic is to get us to believe that they're telling us the truth. Then have kids play the game. After everyone has chosen a side or after eight minutes, have the humans take off their blindfolds to find out which area they went to.

Have kids form trios comprised of an angel, a human, and a demon. Have trios discuss these questions:

● **Do you believe angels and demons really exist? Why or why not?**

● **How did it feel to act as an angel? a demon? a human?**

● **How is this activity like the spiritual battle we are really in? How is it different?**

Then say: **There's a lot of interest in and debate about angels and demons today. Some people completely deny their existence; others have become so impressed and intrigued with angels or demons that they actually worship them. The Bible makes it clear that <u>angels and demons are active in your life.</u> It also presents a view that is accurate and very balanced. Let me show you what I mean.**

DEPTH FINDER   A LOOK AT THE ARMOR

In Ephesians 6:10-18, Paul discusses the armor of God based on the armor that was used during his time. To help your kids understand the analogy that Paul used, consider sharing the following possible parallels between the pieces of armor and the spiritual equivalents:

Belt of Truth: During Paul's day, soldiers used belts to hold up their tunics or to "gird their loins." This was to keep their tunics from getting in the way during battle. In the same way, we must belt ourselves in truth and keep lies from getting in our way during the spiritual war.

Breastplate of Righteousness: Breastplates were used to protect the heart and other vital organs from any arrows that might get past the shield. In the same way, we must live in honesty and humility before God to keep Satan and his demons away from our hearts and souls.

Good News of Peace on Your Feet: Just as good shoes will help a soldier stand true during battle, the Good News of Jesus Christ will help us hold steady against the enemy.

Shield of Faith: The shield was often made of leather and sometimes soaked with water. When flaming arrows hit the shield, the arrows would be stopped and the flame extinguished. Satan often attacks us by causing us to doubt. If our faith is active and strong, his attacks are rendered ineffective.

Helmet of Salvation: Just as helmets protected the soldiers' heads from being injured or crushed under blows from the enemy, our salvation in Jesus Christ keeps Satan from invading and controlling our minds, and ultimately, our lives.

Sword of the Spirit: This is the Word of God. Swords were used by soldiers during Paul's day for offensive and defensive maneuvers. In the same way, a knowledge and understanding of the Word of God helps us defend against and overcome "every proud thing that raises itself against the knowledge of God" (2 Corinthians 10:5).

BIBLE EXPLORATION ▼

Playing With Power (5 to 10 minutes)
Have kids form groups of three by gathering with students who acted the same part in the "War Games" activity. Give each student a pencil, a sheet of paper, and the appropriate section from the "Playing With Power" handout (p. 22). Tell your students that everyone in the group should complete the handout because everyone will be responsible to share the information with others.

When kids finish their handouts or after ten minutes, call them back together. Ask:

● **What did you discover about how <u>angels and demons</u> are active in your life?**

● **According to the Scriptures you looked at, how was our game an inaccurate picture of what spiritual warfare is like? How was it an accurate picture?**

DEPTHFINDER — THE TRUTH ABOUT ANGELS AND DEMONS

The Bible gives clear and specific descriptions of angels and demons. Use the following verses and descriptions to help your kids shatter the myths about angels and demons. **Angels...**

- guide people in times of special need (Genesis 24:7; Acts 8:26).
- minister to and protect those who hurt (1 Kings 19:3-8; Hebrews 1:14).
- provide comfort and strength in times of sorrow and danger (Luke 22:39-44; Acts 27:21-25).
- protect and deliver their charges from harm (Genesis 19:12-17).
- are messengers and instruments of God's will (Matthew 28:1-7; Acts 10:1-8).
- appear in dreams and visions to give warnings and announcements (Luke 1:8-14; Matthew 2:13-21).
- execute God's judgment (Genesis 19:12-13).
- protect people who take a stand for God (Daniel 6:19-22; Acts 12:6-10).

The Devil and Demons...

- deceive people into doubting God (Genesis 3:1-5).
- are created beings, not the spirits of dead humans (Psalm 148:2-5).
- tempt Christians to sin (Ephesians 2:1-3; 1 Thessalonians 3:5).
- seek to keep Christians from growing in their relationships with God (Ephesians 6:11-12).
- hinder Christians in serving God (1 Thessalonians 2:18).
- lead people away from God through deception (1 Timothy 4:1).
- encourage selfishness and jealousy among Christians (James 3:13-15).
- encourage persecution against Christians (Revelation 2:10).

Heavenly Stories (15 to 20 minutes)

Say: **We're going to put into practice the biblical truths your group discovered. I'd like you to get into groups of three. Please make certain your group has one person who acted as a demon, one who acted as an angel, and one who acted as a human. Bring the handout you completed to your group.**

After kids get into their groups, ask a volunteer to read aloud Ephesians 6:12. Have the groups number off from one to four. Give each group an "Unseen Messengers" handout (pp. 23-24), and set paper and pencils in the middle of the room.

Say: **Please follow the directions on the handout I've given your group. Use the story that corresponds with the number of your group. For example, the ones will read and use story number one, the twos will use story number two, and so on.**

Give kids about seven minutes to prepare the re-creations of their stories. Then ask the groups to explain the stories they read and to give their presentations. When the groups finish, ask:

- **Do you think the presentations show an accurate picture of what really happened? Why or why not?**
- **What things, other than angels and demons, may have**

LEADER TIP for Heavenly Stories

If time doesn't permit each group to give its presentation, ask for one group to volunteer its presentation for each of the four stories, or have groups give their presentations simultaneously in different areas of your meeting room.

affected the events and outcomes of the situations?

Say: <u>**Angels and demons are active in your life**</u> **and so**  **is God. God is far greater than all spiritual forces combined. You can be certain that he provides a way for your protection regardless of the plans Satan and demons may have for you. One way he provides for our safety is through spiritual armor. Let me show you what I mean.**

PERSONAL APPLICATION ▼

Armor All (10 to 15 minutes) Have kids get into groups of four. Give each group a sheet of paper and a pencil. Distribute to the groups all seven of the paper strips you made before the study. Ask a volunteer to read aloud Ephesians 6:10-18 while others follow along. Then say: **I've given each group one of the spiritual "pieces" of armor that Paul explains we should put on in preparation for spiritual battle. With your group, find your piece of armor in Ephesians 6:10-18 and write explanations of at least three different ways your piece of armor can be used for protection in spiritual attacks. For example, if your group has "helmet of salvation," you can explain that when you have fears that you might go to hell, you can remember that faith in Christ assures salvation. Or if your group has "feet ready with the gospel of peace," you can explain that when your friend tells you that she thinks all religions are the same, you'll be prepared to explain how the Gospel is unique and true.**

Have kids begin brainstorming their explanations. After five minutes, have kids come back together, and ask for one explanation from each group. Then ask:

● **How does the armor of God protect us from the attacks of the devil?**

● **How can we put on the armor of God?**

Have a volunteer read aloud Philippians 2:9-11.

Say: <u>**Angels and demons are active in your life,**</u> **but they are subject to the power of Jesus. God has provided a way for our protection from evil. Sometimes he sends messages to us through his angels, sometimes his Spirit shows us the way to go, and we can always put on his armor through prayer and reading the Bible.**

As we come to know more truth, walk in righteousness, and grow in our faith, the attacks and deceptions of evil have less of an influence on our lives.

The final instruction Paul gives regarding spiritual armor is to pray and be ready. So I'd like you to find a partner, open your Bibles to Ephesians 6:10-18, and find one of the pieces of your armor that may be weaker than the others. With your partner, pray that God would strengthen you in that area.

Give kids a few minutes to pray, then have partners each share about one piece of armor that they see is especially strong in their partner's life.

LEADER TIP for Armor All

If you have more than twenty-eight students in your group, duplicate one of the seven words on a separate slip of paper for every additional four students. If you have less than twenty-eight students, have groups double up on armor pieces as necessary or form smaller groups.

PLAYING WITH POWER

ANGELS:

Look up the following verses. Under each verse write down what it says about what angels do, what they don't do, and what power they have and don't have:

● Genesis 19:1-22

● Exodus 23:20-23

● Luke 22:39-43

● Hebrews 1:5-7,14

- -

DEMONS:

Look up the following verses. Under each verse write down what it says about what demons do, what they don't do, and what power they have and don't have:

● Matthew 8:28-32

● Matthew 16:21-23

● 1 Peter 5:8-9

● Revelation 12:7-12

- -

HUMANS:

Look up the following verses. Under each verse write down what it says about what part humans have in spiritual warfare including what they do, what they don't do, and what power they have and don't have:

● Luke 10:17-20

● Acts 16:16-18

● Ephesians 6:10-18

● 2 Corinthians 10:3-6

Unseen Messengers

1. Share the information you discovered about angels, demons, or humans with the rest of your group.

2. Read the story that's been assigned to your group.

3. Change the story by either rewriting it, turning it into a short made-for-TV drama, composing a scientific formula that shows what happened, or turning it into an opera. In your re-creation, show what part angels and demons could've had in the story and what someone who could see both the spiritual realm and the physical realm would've observed. Use the information you gathered regarding angels, demons, and humans to guide you in the presentation of the story.

Story Number 1

Courtney Lee Stubbert of Pleasant Hill, Oregon left for home at 11:30 that night. He yawned as he climbed into his '72 Duster to begin the twenty-mile trip. As he was driving, he felt his eyelids getting heavy. "You're almost there," he told himself.

"My fingers loosened their grip on the steering wheel," says Courtney. He fell asleep. Courtney woke up to see his car smash into a concrete bridge abutment. The right side of his car was torn off; the car flipped over and came to a stop. Courtney explains, "Hanging upside down from my seat belt, I felt tiny shards of glass in my eyelashes and hair...'Get out, get out!' an inner voice urged."

Courtney was able to get out and walk away from the Duster before it was engulfed in flames.

—Adapted from "How the Light Rescued Me," *Angels on Earth*, premiere issue

Story Number 2

Sharon headed to the Junior High youth meeting renewed and excited. It was the first meeting since the retreat, and she couldn't wait to see what would happen next. On the way, her mother's car had a flat tire in the rain and no one stopped to help. While they were fixing the flat, Sharon and her mom got into a huge fight. Then, because of the flat, they had to hurry to get to her meeting on time. Once there, Sharon was so frustrated that she not only lost her enthusiasm, but she was short-tempered and couldn't wait for the meeting to end.

Story Number 3

Linda Robinson of Utah woke from a deep sleep at 2:00 in the morning. She explains that she heard a voice saying, "Get up and lock your door." When she woke up she didn't hear a voice, but she felt like she should still lock the door. Linda got out of bed and found that her front door was locked. For some reason, she felt that she should check the kitchen door. Linda explains, "I froze with fear as I saw that the door which we rarely ever opened was, indeed, unlocked." What Linda describes as an internal voice seemed to shout, "Now!"

As Linda locked the door, she heard someone walking in the alley. The person tried to turn the doorknob but found it locked.

—Adapted from *Do Angels Really Exist?* by Dr. David O. Dykes

Story Number 4

Ever since Mike's dad died, Mike had trouble making friends. Since starting at a new school in a new town, Mike spent his school days and his weekends alone. One day, while Mike was sitting alone during lunch, Cindy felt as if she should sit down next to Mike and start a conversation. She walked towards Mike. When she came close to his table, Mike glanced at her. Cindy walked past Mike and sat with her friends. Cindy still felt that she needed to talk with Mike. So halfway through her lunch, she got up and sat down next to him. They began to talk, and Cindy had the opportunity to invite Mike to visit an after-school Bible study.

Face the Music

How Music Affects Kids' Lives

> "When modes of music change, the fundamental laws of the state change with them." —Plato

by Steve Saavedra

■ Music's power was recognized centuries ago by the great Western philosophers. Plato noted that music had such considerable influence that it could, and would, eventually change the laws of the state. Aristotle, noting that "music has the power to form character," wanted to go so far as to see it regulated by the state. Vladimir Lenin, co-founder of communism and one of history's greatest experts on subversion and revolution, understood the sheer power of music to topple societies and said, "One quick way to destroy a society is through its music." ■ If the great philosophers and revolutionaries are correct about the nature of music, what effects might today's music be having on the hearts and minds of today's teenagers? This study will help your students begin an honest evaluation of the music they choose to listen to. ■ (Source: *Hell's Bells: The Dangers of Rock 'n' Roll* video, Reel to Real Ministries)

THE POINT:

We're spiritual as well as physical beings.

The Study
AT A GLANCE

SECTION	MINUTES	WHAT STUDENTS WILL DO	SUPPLIES
Opener	10 to 15	SOUL MUSIC—Listen to contemporary music and analyze the emotions it evokes.	Cassette or CD player, two prerecorded songs
Affirmative Exploration	5 to 10	BRAINWASH—List the messages in the songs they listen to. Then "brainwash" each other with positive affirmations, and through debriefing see the effect positive and negative messages can have on them.	Paper, pencils, newsprint, markers
Digging Deeper	25 to 30	QUOTES TO NOTE—Give presentations about the spiritual effects of music on the soul after examining Scripture and other noteworthy quotes.	Bibles, "Quotes to Note" handouts (pp. 33-35), paper, pencils
Closing	5 to 10	GUARD YOUR HEART—Describe their commitment to guard their hearts by rewriting a lyric or song title.	Bibles, index cards, pencils

notes: Music - The science or art of pleasing, expressive, or intelligibile combination of tones.
Sing - to produce musical tones by means of voice
" " harmonious sounds, as those made by birds & brooks
to make a small shrill sound - missles sing through the air
to relate or celebrate something in poetry
to hum to ring
* to utter w/ musical inflections
* to celebrate in song or verse
to chant intone

We're spiritual as well as physical beings.

THE BIBLE CONNECTION

I SAMUEL 16:14-23	David is summoned to play the harp for King Saul.
EPHESIANS 5:1-11	Paul explains that we should live like children who belong to the light.
EPHESIANS 6:12-13	Paul explains that we are fighting a spiritual battle.
PHILIPPIANS 4:8	Paul admonishes the Philippians to think about things that are good.

I n this study, kids will listen to music and think critically about the lyrics behind the music they listen to. Through a presentation, they'll teach their classmates what they've discovered about the negative and positive effects of music on their spiritual lives. Students will be given an opportunity to make a commitment regarding their future choices of music.

Through this experience, kids will learn that music affects their spiritual lives.

Explore the verses in The Bible Connection, then examine the information in the Depthfinder boxes throughout the study to gain a deeper understanding of how these Scriptures connect with your young people.

BEFORE THE STUDY

For the "Soul Music" activity, obtain a cassette or CD with a contemporary song that has a negative, rebellious, or depressing message—such as Soundgarden's "The Day I Tried to Live" or Green Day's "Having a Blast." Also obtain a cassette or CD with a song that has an uplifting or positive message—such as "Love Song for a Savior" by Jars of Clay. Make certain that both songs are as contemporary as possible.

Photocopy one "Quotes to Note" handout (pp. 33-35) for every twelve students in your class and cut the handout into three sections.

LEADER TIP for The Study

Because this topic can be so powerful and relevant to kids' lives, your group members may be tempted to get caught up in issues and lose sight of the deeper biblical principle found in The Point. Help your kids grasp The Point by guiding kids to focus on the biblical investigation and discussing how God's truth connects with reality in their lives.

THE STUDY

OPENER ▼

LEADER TIP

for Soul Music

To make certain you don't play obscene or offensive songs for your class, read the lyrics to the songs you plan to use or listen to the music before the study.

Soul Music (10 to 15 minutes)

As kids arrive, have contemporary Christian music playing in the background. Have kids get in pairs to discuss the following questions:

● **Tell about a time a song really affected you. What song was it?**
● **How did it make you feel?**
● **What was the basic message of the lyrics?**
● **Why does music affect people in such a way?**

When kids finish their discussions, say: **Please close your eyes and listen to the song I'm about to play. As you listen, pay close attention to the mood of the song and what the songwriter is trying to communicate.**

Play the song you obtained before the study that has negative lyrics. Then ask kids to open their eyes. Discuss the song with your students by asking three or four questions that are especially appropriate on the following list from *Understanding Today's Youth Culture* by Walt Mueller.

● **What does this song say about humanity?**
● **What does the song say about happiness and where it comes from?**
● **Is the song hopeful or hopeless?**
● **Are solutions offered to life's problems? If so, what are they?**
● **What character traits are promoted as positive? negative?**
● **How is beauty and personal worth defined?**
● **What does the song say about the nature of sexuality?**
● **What does it say about God?**
● **What values or world views are behind the lyrics?**

After you've discussed the three or four questions you chose, ask:

● **Did the song affect your mood? Explain.**
● **If somebody listened to this song over and over again, could it affect him or her emotionally? Why or why not?**
● **Would it affect them spiritually? Explain.**

LEADER TIP

for Soul Music

To make certain the music you play is relevant and acceptable to your group, ask your students for suggestions before the study. If you don't have access to the cassettes or CDs they suggest, ask your students to let you borrow them.

Play the song you obtained before the study that has positive lyrics. Ask kids to close their eyes as the song plays. Debrief the experience the same way you did for the first song.

Then say: **Music has the power to affect our emotions. Parents usually don't play hard rock music to lull their babies to sleep. Athletes usually don't listen to lullabies before they compete. Both parents and athletes know that certain types of music evoke certain types of emotions. But because <u>we're spiritual as well as physical beings,</u> these emotions can also influence our spirits. Despair, discouragement, joy, bitterness, and anger can all be conditions of the spirit. Music can feed or fight all**

DEPTHFINDER — THE POWER OF MUSIC

LEADER TIP for The Study

Whenever you ask groups to discuss a list of questions, write the questions on newsprint and tape the newsprint to the wall so groups can answer the questions at their own pace.

Dr. David Elkind, in his book *Hurried Child: Growing up Too Fast Too Soon*, says, "One of the most underestimated influences on young people today is the music industry." The National Review echoes Elkind's remark: "Rock's sheer pervasiveness makes it the most profound values-shaper in existence today. Unless you are deaf, it's virtually guaranteed that rock music has affected your view of the world."

Studies show that the average teenager will listen to and watch 11,000 hours of rock music and videos, more than twice the time he or she will spend in class. Other studies indicate that the average teenager watches somewhere between thirty minutes to two hours of music videos a day.

Walt Mueller, in his book *Understanding Today's Youth Culture*, says "Music interprets and defines life for teenagers. It suggests legitimate and proper responses to the different situations, problems, and opportunities that teenagers will face each day. It serves to define the meaning of life, values, attitudes, behavioral norms, and social and gender roles. Music has become a powerful socialization authority for teens."

As you teach this lesson, try to help your kids see the profound impact music has on their lives. Kids may explain that they don't follow what the music says, with arguments such as, "I'm not going to go out and kill someone just because a song says to." Concede to that point, and try to help kids see the subtle ways music affects their lives. Ask questions such as, "Can music affect your mood?" "What kinds of music do you study to?" "Why don't you study to other kinds of music?" and "What kinds of music do skaters/people in gangs/people in other 'groups' listen to? Why do they listen to that type of music?"

(Sources: *Hell's Bells: The Dangers of Rock 'n' Roll* video, Reel to Real Ministries and *Understanding Today's Youth Culture* by Walt Mueller)

of these feelings. In this lesson we'll explore the effects music can have on our spirits and how we can be more selective about the music we listen to.

AFFIRMATIVE EXPLORATION ▼

Brainwash (5 to 10 minutes) Have kids form groups of four. Give each group paper and a pencil. Give groups thirty seconds to write down every band they can think of. While they work, tape a sheet of newsprint to the wall and put markers on the floor. Then ask kids to list the main message each of the bands gives to its listeners. After three minutes, have kids choose the three messages that popular music in general talks about the most. Have each group use one of the markers to write its top three messages on the sheet of newsprint.

Then say: **Studies say that the average teenager listens to four to six hours of music a day. Do you think this is true or false?** Talk through an average day with the class and ask them to make a mental

"The key to winning this battle lies in understanding how personal this music is; it goes right for our kids' hearts. Their music can reveal inner struggles and needs; it can reveal the spiritual and moral health of a child; it can reflect doubts and fears, and even spotlight the happy places in their lives."—Al Menconi, quoted in *Understanding Today's Youth Culture* by Walt Mueller

As you talk about music with your kids, remember that it's an intensely personal subject for them. Be careful to remain objective and nonjudgmental. Try to let the kids draw their own conclusions and be aware that mishandling this subject could drastically damage your rapport with kids.

But don't be intimidated. Kids need to examine their music with your guidance. Explain that your objective isn't to condemn musicians or those who listen to them but to help the group take an honest look at an important part of their lives. Encourage kids to keep open minds, and let them know that you'll do the same.

note of how many hours they spend listening to music. Be sure to include times such as getting ready for school, drive time, after-school activities, study time and going to sleep.

After they've determined how many hours of music they listen to a day, have students find a partner. Say: **Now I want us to experience the effects of listening to a positive message for just a fraction of the time you probably listen to music. Think about a positive or encouraging thing to say to your partner. For example, you could say, "You make others feel welcome." Now, starting with whoever's birthday is closest to New Year's, turn to your partner and say that statement over and over again for thirty seconds. You can't pause, and I'm going to time you. Ready? Go!**

After thirty seconds have kids switch roles. Then ask:
- **How did it feel to give the positive message?**
- **How did it feel to receive the message?**
- **How would it affect you if, for the same number of hours you listen to music each day, people gave you that message?**
- **How do you think it would affect your self-esteem if people said negative things to you that many hours a day?**
- **How is this activity like the effects our choices of music might have on us? How is it different?**

Review the list of messages on the newsprint by asking students how each message might affect a person's spirit.

Then say: **Because <u>we're spiritual as well as physical beings,</u> we need to be very conscientious about the musical messages we take in. Positive messages in music can build up our understanding of what it means to follow God in this confusing world. Negative messages only serve to confuse us more, hide the hopeful message of the Gospel, and chip away at our spiritual well-being. As Christians we need to learn to think critically about the kinds of music we choose to listen to.**

DIGGING DEEPER ▼

Quotes to Note (25 to 30 minutes)
Have kids form three groups. Give a different section of the "Quotes to Note" handout (pp. 33-35) to each group. Ask groups to follow the directions on their handouts. Set paper and pencils in the middle of the room for kids to use for their presentations.

Give each group about ten minutes to read and prepare their presentations. Have group members read their corresponding quotes and Bible passages to the class. Then have each group give its presentations to the rest of the class.

Say: **Because <u>we're spiritual as well as physical beings,</u> music can have positive and negative effects on our attitudes, our behaviors, and our spiritual lives. A relationship with God is precious and can be helped or hindered by music. Many things, including music, can distract our spirits and keep us from experiencing a full, meaningful, and intimate friendship with our God. The Bible encourages us to guard our hearts, thoughts, and souls against forces that wish to get between us and God. These forces can be anything from sexually perverse thoughts to rebellious attitudes—all of which we can find in popular music today.**

CLOSING ▼

Guard Your Heart (5 to 10 minutes)
Ask kids to form trios and read Proverbs 4:23 together. Then ask them to discuss how they can guard their hearts when it comes to music. Encourage kids to go beyond generalizations and to come up with specific examples. For example, instead of concluding that they should avoid all music that contains profanity, students should decide what to do when friends play music that is vulgar. After a few minutes have them report their ideas back to the class.

LEADER TIP for Quotes to Note

If you have more than twelve students in your class, photocopy the handout enough times for every four students to have one section. Have the three groups form subgroups so that no group has more than four students. Either have kids make their presentations while other presentations are going on, or choose one group to give its presentation for each section of the handout.

"Our fight is not against people on earth but against the rulers and authorities and the powers of this world's darkness, against the spiritual powers of evil in the heavenly world." —Ephesians 6:12

DEPTHFINDER

TIMES (AND TUNES) HAVE CHANGED

According to Walt Mueller's *Understanding Today's Youth Culture*, the power of media has dramatically increased over the last three decades. Notice where he ranks media on the following three lists:

Institutions which had the most influence on the values and behaviors of teenagers in 1960, in order:

1) family
2) school
3) friends and peers
4) church

Institutions which had the most influence on the values and behaviors of teenagers in 1980, in order:

1) friends and peers
2) family
3) media
4) school

Institutions which have the most influence on the values and behaviors of teenagers in 1994, in order:

1) media
2) friends and peers
3) family
4) school

Then ask kids to each find a spot in the room where they can be by themselves, and give each person an index card and a pencil.

Say: **We're going to have a time of prayerful reflection and recommitment. I encourage you to ask God to help you decide if you listen to any music that hinders your relationship with him. Then make a commitment to guard your heart against it and find an adequate substitute. For example, for one week you might consider creating five minutes of silence for yourself every day, or you might choose to turn off music as you get ready for school just to see how it affects you. To express this commitment, reword a title or lyric from one of your favorite songs or choose a Christian song you are familiar with. Write your lyric or title on your index card. Take the index card home with you to serve as a reminder that <u>we're spiritual as well as physical beings</u> and that music does affect us.**

Allow a few minutes for kids to think, write, and pray. Encourage them to be silent as they work. Then close with a group prayer asking God to help them be more conscientious about the music they listen to in order to protect their hearts, minds, and souls.

Quotes to Note

1. Read these quotes from some popular (and not so popular) musicians:

"One night we were playing and suddenly the spirit entered into me, and I was playing, but it was no longer me playing."

> **—John McLaughlin, secular jazz guitarist**

"Joni Mitchell's own strongest creative impulses come to her in a somewhat unusual way. She deeply believes in a male muse named Art, who lends her his key to what she airily calls, 'the shrine of creativity.' "

> **— Article about Joni Mitchell, secular folk/jazz artist**
> **(Time magazine)**

"I guess my strength comes from some green laser beam in outer space or somewhere. When I'm onstage, I plug into another power source that's all-encompassing. My whole religious experience happens right there in those two hours."

> **— Chaka Khan, secular musician**
> **("Women Who Rock!" Interview magazine, November 1996)**

"I do believe that music itself is a spiritual force. The inspiration I feel is like a holy thing. It's beyond any words I can use to describe it."

> **— Peter Rowan, secular musician**
> **(Washington Post)**

"Someone else is steering me, I'm just along for the ride. I become possessed when I'm on stage."

> **— Angus Young, secular musician**
> **(Hit Parader, 1985)**

2. Discuss the following questions with your group:

● According to these musicians, who inspires their music?
● Who or what do *you* think inspires the musicians?
● Read Ephesians 6:12-13. Do you think some music is influenced by "forces of darkness"? Why or why not? If so, what characteristics would such music have?
● Is it possible for music to be inspired by good spiritual forces? Why or why not? If so, what characteristics would such music have?
● How can we know what music we should and shouldn't listen to?

3. Prepare a presentation in the form of a skit, a song you write and perform on "instruments" around the room (such as a garbage can), or anything else you can think of. In your skit or song, show or tell about a rock musician or band who receives inspiration for songs from spiritual forces. Use some of the quotes for ideas. Also show how the messages the musicians receive "from beyond" can influence a teenage listener.

1. Read these quotes from some people who were or are heavily involved in music:

"Music is the language of languages. It can be said that of all the arts, there is none that more powerfully moves or changes the consciousness."

> —**David Tame, musicologist**

"The end of all music should be the glory of God and the refreshment of the human spirit."

> —**J.S. Bach, German composer**

Music is…"the perfect expression of the soul."

> —**Robert Schumann, German composer**

2. Discuss the following questions with your group:

- According to the quotes you just read, what purpose does music serve? What power does it have?
- Read I Samuel 16:14-23. What was Saul's problem and what was the temporary solution?
- David eventually became the King of Israel and is called later in the Bible "a man after God's own heart." Based on this and anything else you know about David, why do you think the evil spirit left Saul when David played his harp?
- What does this passage say about music?
- Read Philippians 4:8. What kinds of lyrical themes or messages fit the criteria presented in this verse?

3. Prepare a presentation in the form of a skit, a song you write and perform on "instruments" around the room (such as a garbage can), or anything else you can think of. In your skit or song, illustrate how music can be used in a beneficial way. For example, show or tell about a rock musician or band who plays music that honors God and helps people. Use the quotes and Scripture verses to guide the message of your presentation.

1. Read these quotes from some people who were or are heavily involved in music:

"Music is used everywhere to condition the human mind. It can be just as powerful as a drug and much more dangerous, because nobody takes musical manipulation very seriously."

> **—Eddy Manson, composer**

"I can explain everything better through music. You hypnotize people to where they go right back to their natural state and when you get people at their weakest point, you can preach into the subconscious what we want to say."

> **— Jimi Hendrix, secular musician**
> **(Life magazine, 1969)**

"Music! What a wonderful medium! Music can be so incredibly destructive, but it can also be so incredibly life-giving."

> **—Ashley Cleveland, singer/songwriter**
> **(Contemporary Christian Music magazine, July 1996)**

2. Discuss the following questions with your group:

- Do you think music is powerful? Why or why not?
- Are there certain types of music we should avoid? If so, what are they?
- Read Ephesians 5:1-12. According to this passage, how can we evaluate what music we should listen to?
- Do you believe music can eventually affect the way teenagers understand love and human relationships? Why or why not?
- Do you think Paul's advice in verse 4 applies in any way to the music industry? Why or why not?
- How do you think Paul's advice applies to the music choices of teenagers?

3. Prepare a presentation in the form of a skit, a song you write and perform on "instruments" around the room (such as a garbage can), or anything else you can think of. In your skit or song, show or tell the story of a teenager who is confused by the countless messages in music. Have the character make a choice and show what the biblical consequences of that choice are. For example, in your presentation you could demonstrate the life of a teenager in a dilemma because he or she is receiving mixed messages about romantic love. At home and at church that person is told that real romantic love is unconcerned with self, entirely giving, and is ultimately experienced within the bounds of marriage. But on the radio and at school, the person hears that love takes whatever makes it feel good, is unconcerned about the feelings of another, and should be experienced through sex as much and as soon as possible.

(Source: All quotes in this handout, unless otherwise noted, are from the video
Hell's Bells: The Dangers of Rock 'n' Roll, Reel to Real Ministries.)

Feast or Famine

by Rick Lawrence

HELPING KIDS FIND TRUE SPIRITUAL NOURISHMENT

THE POINT:

Not everything spiritual is good.

■ Life, for many kids in junior high, is dominated by new and unusual forms of pain they must find a way to weather: brutal rejections, embarrassing physical changes, growing academic pressures, parental conflict, social isolation, violence, and on and on. Pain has a loud voice that demands relief. We all want the quickest route to comfort, and we instinctively move away from pain. God doesn't promise to always take our pain away. He does, however, offer a way through pain if we just look to him for healing and help. ■ Drugs, on the other hand, promise to camouflage and deaden pain in the short-term—and that's a powerful temptation. In this sense, drugs offer a counterfeit path to spiritual peace. The path is often shorter than the one laid out by God, but it leads to a cliff. And more and more kids are jumping off that cliff. According to Group Magazine, during a recent three-year stretch, the number of drug-abusing teenagers almost doubled. ■ This study will help kids discover the hidden dangers of the counterfeit drug-path to spiritual peace. It will give them a taste of God's goodness as they learn to trust him with the pain and fear they face as they venture onto the path he's put before them.

The Study
AT A GLANCE

SECTION	MINUTES	WHAT STUDENTS WILL DO	SUPPLIES
Learning Game	10 to 15	GOOD-FOR-YOU SCAVENGER HUNT—Discuss and vote on whether specific things are always good or always bad for us.	Paper, pencils
Bible Exploration	20 to 25	NAME THAT DRUG—Explore the uses of some legal drugs, then discover some of God's "prescriptions" by studying Bible passages.	Bibles, paper, pencils, prescription or over-the-counter drug boxes or bottles
Bible Reflection	10 to 15	THE SODA POP ABUSE—Learn what it's like when a harmless-sounding activity turns into a negative experience.	Bibles, bowl of pretzels, soft drinks, large cups of water, paper, pencils
Closing Story	5 to 10	TELL ME A STORY—Listen to a story about a real experience with drugs and compare it to Scripture.	Bibles

notes:

Not everything spiritual is good.

THE BIBLE CONNECTION

DEUTERONOMY 32:39	God explains that he can bring hurt and healing.
ISAIAH 40:28-31	God promises strength and freedom for those who will wait for him to show his goodness.
GALATIANS 5:16-26	Paul tells the Galatians that the flesh and the Spirit are at war and encourages the Galatians to let the Spirit lead them.
EPHESIANS 5:15-20	Paul tells the Ephesians how to live wisely.

I n this study, kids will go on a scavenger hunt to find things that seem to be good and discuss how the things can be used for bad. They'll investigate the purposes of legal drugs and compare their findings to the impact of illegal drugs, participate in an experience that shows how things that look good can actually be destructive, and listen to a real-life drug-related tragedy.

Through this experience, kids will discover how drugs are a poor, destructive substitute for the good things God wants to give us.

Explore the verses in The Bible Connection, then examine the information in the Depthfinder boxes throughout the study to gain a deeper understanding of how these Scriptures connect with your young people.

BEFORE THE STUDY

Collect one empty box or bottle for prescription or over-the-counter drugs for every three students in your group. Make certain the boxes and bottles include the drugs' directions and applications.

LEADER TIP for The Study

Because this topic can be so powerful and relevant to kids' lives, your group members may be tempted to get caught up in issues and lose sight of the deeper biblical principle found in The Point. Help your kids grasp The Point by guiding kids to focus on the biblical investigation and discussing how God's truth connects with reality in their lives.

THE STUDY

LEARNING GAME ▼

LEADER TIP

for Good-for-You Scavenger Hunt

To personalize this activity, come up with your own list of things or actions for kids to vote on, but make certain "drugs" is the last item on your list.

Good-for-You Scavenger Hunt (10 to 15 minutes)

Have kids form two teams. Tell kids on Team 1 that their challenge is to find objects in your youth room or church that are "good for you." Tell kids on Team 2 that their challenge is to take each object Team 1 presents and find at least one reason "it's not good for you." Give Team 1 a minute to find and present an object. Then give Team 2 a minute to come up with as many reasons as possible that the object is not always good. Have Team 2 list each reason and discuss it with Team 1.

After teams repeat the challenge three times, ask:

● **Was it easier to find things that are always good for you or to point out why the things aren't always good? Why?**

● **Is there anything in life that is *always* good for you? If so, what?**

Say: **Let's further explore this question. Imagine the left side of our room represents "never good for you," the right side of the room represents "always good for you," and the space in the middle of the room represents "sometimes good, sometimes bad for you." When I say a word, I want you to vote on whether that thing or activity is always, never, or sometimes good for you. Vote by standing somewhere between the walls.**

Say each of the following words, and have kids vote on each word. After each vote, ask one student from the left, middle, and right side of the room to explain why he or she voted that way. Say:

- ● **ice cream**
- ● **exercise**
- ● **MTV**
- ● **knowledge**
- ● **sports**
- ● **success**
- ● **good looks**
- ● **friends**
- ● **drugs**

After kids have voted on each word, say: **Many people think illegal drugs are always or sometimes good for you. Drugs, according to rock star Evan Dando of the Lemonheads, "make you feel good for no reason." Drugs, to some people, are a quick way to forget about their troubles and feel good. But God has ways to help us deal with our troubles too. Drugs offer a counterfeit way to find the kind of spiritual comfort and peace God wants to give us. In our meeting today, we'll explore why <u>not everything spiritual is good</u>.**

BIBLE EXPLORATION ▼

Name That Drug (20 to 25 minutes)

Have kids form groups of three, and give each group paper, pencils, and one of the drug bottles or boxes that you collected before the study. Have each group choose a captain, a recorder, and a reporter. Explain that the captains are responsible for making certain that all the questions are answered, the recorders are responsible for writing down the groups' discoveries, and the reporters are responsible for explaining to the rest of the class what the groups found. Ask groups to investigate the purposes, restrictions, and dangers of their drugs by discussing the following questions:

● **What's the primary purpose of this drug?**
● **What side effects does it have?**
● **What could happen if someone took this medicine inappropriately?**
● **How is this drug like an illegal drug such as cocaine, heroin, LSD, or marijuana?**
● **How is it unlike an illegal drug?**

Have the reporters explain their groups' discoveries to the rest of the class. Then ask:

● **Why do people take prescription or over-the-counter drugs?**
● **Why do people take illegal drugs?**
● **How is an illegal drug abuser different from a person who uses prescription or over-the-counter drugs?**
● **How are they similar?**

Ask a volunteer to read aloud Deuteronomy 32:39. Then say: **People often call God "the Great Physician." Since God is all-powerful, he understands our struggles and our pains and has a "prescription" for them. In fact, God has given us prescriptions throughout the Bible for our pain. Here's one:**

LEADER TIP
for Name That Drug

If kids have difficulty finding prescriptions in their assigned books, point them to specific chapters. While just about all of the chapters will work, Galatians 3; Ephesians 4; Philippians 2; and Colossians 2 are especially appropriate.

DEPTHFINDER — UNDERSTANDING PARENTS

According to a recent USA Today article, James Copple of the Community Anti-Drug Coalitions of America asserts that almost two-thirds of your kids' parents used drugs in the '60s, and that makes talking to their kids about drugs especially difficult for them. Because so many parents used drugs, they feel a moral conflict when it comes to warning their kids about drugs. The sad result is that many kids aren't hearing a clear message about the dangers of drug abuse from people who can significantly shape their beliefs.

Break the ice by planning a parents-only meeting on teenage drug abuse. Ask the parents to help you brainstorm discussion questions they can use with their kids. Compile the questions, and send a copy to each parent.

LEADER TIP
for The Study

Whenever groups discuss a list of questions, write the questions on newsprint and tape the newsprint to the wall so groups can discuss the questions at their own pace.

Have kids follow along as a volunteer reads aloud Ephesians 5:15-20. Ask:

● **What "prescriptions" is God telling us to take in this Scripture passage?**

● **What are the prescriptions for?**

● **If you take God's prescriptions, how will they affect your life?**

● **How is the impact of God's prescriptions different from the impact of illegal drugs?**

Then ask groups to each choose the book of Galatians, Ephesians, Philippians, or Colossians and find at least one of God's prescriptions in the book they have selected. Explain that each group will need to decide what the prescription is and what it's for. After five minutes, have kids report what they've found to the rest of the group. Then ask:

● **What's different about these prescriptions compared to the drug prescriptions we studied earlier?**

● **What kinds of spiritual wounds or illnesses are these prescriptions designed to help?**

● **If someone takes illegal drugs to treat these spiritual wounds instead, what will happen?**

● **If God has given us these prescriptions, why do people choose to use illegal drugs instead?**

● **What generally happens to people when they use other prescriptions for spiritual peace instead of God's prescriptions?**

Say: **Remember when I told you that Evan Dando of the Lemonheads said drugs "make you feel good for no reason"? Well, listen to the rest of what Dando said. A Rolling Stone reporter asked him if he was abusing dope. Dando replied: "That stuff's the closest thing to Satan on this planet, because it makes you feel good for no reason. You should feel good for reasons."**

Ask:

● **What do you think about Dando's comparison of drugs to Satan—how are drugs like and unlike Satan?**

Then say: **God knows we have spiritual wounds and sicknesses that need to be healed. He knows we want to feel good about our lives, but sometimes don't. Obviously, we don't have to take God's prescription for our pain. We can take other prescriptions that will make us temporarily forget or hide those pains. When we do, we're substituting our own spiritual treatment for God's spiritual treatment. But remember, <u>not everything spiritual is good.</u>**

BIBLE REFLECTION ▼

The Soda Pop Abuse

(10 to 15 minutes)
Put a bowl of pretzels in the middle of the room, and invite kids to grab a handful. As kids eat the pretzels, set out an assortment of soft drinks. Say: **You can all take a soft drink but don't open it yet. I need two groups of volunteers. The first group of volunteers will get to drink its soft drinks immediately. The**

LEADER TIP
for The Soda Pop Abuse

If you'd rather not use soft drinks for this activity, consider using Kool-Aid or sports drinks. Have kids drink approximately sixteen ounces in ten seconds.

The list of popular rock groups that have been linked to drug abuse reads like a who's who of artists popular with junior highers. According to a recent Newsweek article, the list includes Nirvana, Hole, Smashing Pumpkins, Everclear, Blind Melon, Skinny Puppy, Red Hot Chili Peppers, Stone Temple Pilots, the Breeders, Alice in Chains, Depeche Mode—and this is just a sampling. Because rock stars set the standard for what's popular in youth culture, their drug abuse is often seen by kids as the ultimate path to respect and freedom.

You may encounter resistance as you discuss the negative aspects of drugs. But it's important to realize that you may be asking kids to do more than change a habit. You may be asking them to change a lifestyle and what they perceive to be their very identity. Drugs affect a user's choices in music, friends, clothing, activities, and most of the other things that teenagers consider important to who they are.

But don't be discouraged. You may be the only voice teenagers care about that goes against the messages they receive from music and the rest of their world. You may be the only link to true freedom for your kids.

second group of volunteers will have to wait about ten minutes before drinking its soft drinks. I'd like all the people who volunteer to drink immediately to go the left side of the room and those who will wait to go to the right side.

Say to the students who volunteered to drink immediately: **Before you drink your soft drink, you must drink a glass of water.** Give each of the students in this group a cup with about sixteen ounces of water and ask all of them to drink the water as fast as they can.

Then say: **When I say "go," you must drink your soft drink as fast as you can. I will count down from ten, and I expect you to have your soft drink finished when I reach zero. Those who volunteered to wait can watch and eat some more pretzels. Are you ready? Go!**

Count down from ten. If students aren't finished when you reach zero, tell them to hurry and finish their drinks. Then have kids form groups of four by pairing with someone from the opposite group then pairing with another pair. Have foursomes discuss:

● **What choice did you make regarding the soft drinks?**
● **Why did you make that choice?**
● **How did you feel when you found out that you had to drink the water before you could have your soft drink?**
● **What negative effects did the choice to drink the soft drink immediately have?**
● **What are some negative effects of drug use?**
● **What are some unexpected effects of drug use?**
● **Are you glad you chose to wait to drink your soft drink? Why or why not?**
● **Is the word "wait" a positive or negative word? Explain.**
● **Why is it sometimes difficult to wait for God to heal our emotional pain?**

LEADER TIP

for The Soda Pop Abuse

If all the students volunteer for the same group, split the group in half, and have the designated "volunteers" go to the other side of the room.

LEADER TIP

for The Soda Pop Abuse

Ask students who are diabetic or have other health issues to volunteer to wait to drink their soft drinks. Consider providing sugar-free drinks as an alternative for your students with health issues.

DEPTHFINDER UNDERSTANDING THE BIBLE

The Hebrew name Satan means accuser or adversary. He has often been caricatured as a quasi-comedic scamp wearing red spandex and carrying a pitchfork. Theologian R.C. Sproul says, "That image, at least in part, arose out of the medieval church. The silly picture of Satan was intentionally created by the church in order to poke fun at him. The church was convinced that an effective ploy to withstand Satan was to insult him. His most vulnerable part was seen as his pride."

The Bible's view of Satan, however, is much more sophisticated. He is often described as an "angel of light." He often presents himself as good so he can delude, then destroy, people. Drugs have the same effect.

As Kent Nerburn says in his book *Letters to My Son*: "Who can deny the thrill of cocaine, the mysticism of peyote and mescaline, methedrine's sense of mastery, or any of the other drug-induced experiences that seem to lift life so far beyond the ordinary?

"Drugs and alcohol are not, in themselves, dark and abysmal horrors. But they carry the seeds of dark and abysmal horrors, and they plant them in your mind, your heart, your very chemical makeup. No matter how benign they seem, no matter how elevated the experience they create, they are giving you something at the expense of something else. They are a devil's bargain—a promise of power in exchange for a service yet unnamed."

● **How do people get into trouble when they refuse to wait for something?**

Give each group paper and a pencil. Say: With your group, read Isaiah 40:28-31. Then list as many ways as you can think of that you've benefited from waiting for something or someone.

After two minutes, ask for volunteers to read aloud their lists. Then say: **Waiting often seems like a negative thing to us, but even in our own lives we can see how waiting has been beneficial. In fact, many people say that the best things in life, including God's prescriptions for our pain, take time. People who abuse drugs refuse to wait for God's best, so they often get the worst of life instead. Remember, <u>not everything spiritual is good.</u> Waiting for God's best is worth it. Pray with your group, asking God for the strength, courage, and wisdom to wait for God's help in life and resist the temptation of drugs.**

After kids finish praying, invite the students who chose to wait to drink their soft drinks to enjoy the beverages as a reminder of the good things that happen when we wait.

CLOSING STORY ▼

Tell Me a Story (5 to 10 minutes)

Say: **Listen while I tell you a true story as reported in a Newsweek article titled "The New Pot Culture": When Kevin West was 17, he and his friends decided to spend an** evening moving from friend's house to friend's house to smoke marijuana. "I felt I could stand out if I did crazy things," says Kevin, who lives in Little Rock. High on marijuana, Kevin agreed to play a game of Russian roulette with a loaded .38-caliber pistol. He spun the chamber, put the gun to his head, and pulled the trigger. Kevin says if he hadn't been high, he would've taken his finger off the trigger. "But on weed you can't think straight," he says. The next thing he knew, he was lying on the ground in a pool of blood, a hole the size of a golf ball in his head. After three operations and months of physical therapy, Kevin remains paralyzed on his left side and takes anti-seizure drugs every day. He remarked: "I only smoked for a few months. Now I'm on drugs for the rest of my life. I thought marijuana was no big deal."

Have kids return to their foursomes to discuss:

● **If you had to choose one word to describe Kevin, what would it be?**

● **Read Galatians 5:16-26. How does this passage relate to Kevin's experience?**

● **How would Kevin's story be different if he had "lived by the Spirit"?**

● **Which of the "things the sinful self does" in verses 19-21 do drugs lead to?**

● **Which of the "fruits of the spirit" in verses 22-23 do drugs lead to?**

Say: **The choices you make have an effect on who you are and who you become. Every choice you make will either produce fruits of the Spirit or fruits of darkness. As Kent Nerburn says in his book** *Letters to My Son:* **"In my youth, when I did a lot of drugs, I always said that they moved my life from black and white to Technicolor. They gave me insights that changed me…All was new and full of joy. Then slowly, I saw it all turn. Words would escape me…I felt vague pains in my body and vague fears overtook my mind…Soon a friend died. Other friends began coughing up blood. One lost his mind…Something was taken from us even as something was given to us. We have a knowledge, but it was not without a price."**

If you choose to experiment with drugs, it's possible that you'll survive without much damage. But when you give up control to drugs, a variety of horrific results of sin can follow. If you don't believe me, ask Kevin West. He learned the hard way that <u>**not everything spiritual is good.**</u>

Heaven on Earth

by Janice Long

THE POINT:

Heaven is real.

■ Teenagers believe in heaven. In fact, a USA Today article reporting on a Gallup Youth Survey states that 91 percent of teenagers profess that heaven exists. But what do they believe *about* heaven? One person muses on America Online that heaven is "the state in which your inner self is at perfect peace" and others jest that it's a place with "harps, angels, and lots of cheese."

■ What do your kids think? Do they believe the reality of heaven affects their everyday lives? This belief is vital because the reality of heaven reminds us of our purpose. Look at it this way—the Christian life without hope of heaven would be like having to go to school for twelve years without knowing you'll eventually graduate. Kids need to know that what they're doing now, day in and day out, has value and meaning—that their efforts are reaching some logical conclusion. ■ That's the way it is with heaven. Our lives here on earth and what we go through here on earth have value when we see it within the context of heaven. What we do here matters for eternity. This is an idea your kids will welcome and embrace. Use this study to help your kids discover that heaven is real and the reality of heaven can affect their everyday lives.

heaven earth

The Study
AT A GLANCE

SECTION	MINUTES	WHAT STUDENTS WILL DO	SUPPLIES
Opener	15 to 20	MY PERSONAL HEAVEN—Compare ideas about heaven.	Bibles, "Heaven's Like This" handouts (p. 55), pencils
Learning Game	10 to 15	IT'S FOR REAL—Participate in a game to see how objects and events in life shape their character.	Bible, paper, pencils, newsprint, marker, tape
Creative Bible Exploration	15 to 20	LATE NIGHT WITH BIBLE CHARACTERS—Make top-ten lists about characters who did and didn't keep focused on heavenly things.	Bibles, index cards, pencils, "Heaven Bound" handouts (p. 56)
Closing	5 to 10	WHAT'S REALLY IMPORTANT?—Evaluate the lasting value of things they cherish, and write a prayer of commitment to God.	Bible, "valuable" things kids bring in, paper, pencils, cross

notes:

Heaven is real.

THE BIBLE CONNECTION

GENESIS 12:1-9; 1 KINGS 3:1-15	These passages tell of events when people had their eyes and hearts focused on heavenly things.
ISAIAH 65:17-25; REVELATION 7:9-11; 21:2-7	These passages describe qualities of heaven or things that will take place in heaven.
MATTHEW 6:19-24	This passage encourages us to keep our hearts set on heaven.
MATTHEW 26:14-16, 47-50; 27:1-10; LUKE 12:13-21	These passages tell of events when people had their eyes and hearts focused on earthly things.
1 CORINTHIANS 3:10-15	This passage tells how our deeds will be judged on the last day.

In this study, kids will evaluate quotes about heaven, investigate the reality of heaven by playing a game, participate in a talk show about character, and make a commitment regarding their own experiences.

By doing this, kids can learn that the choices they make on earth will affect their eternal existence. They can discover that heaven is real and it is relevant to their everyday lives.

Explore the verses in The Bible Connection, then examine the information in the Depthfinder boxes throughout the study to gain a deeper understanding of how these Scriptures connect with your young people.

LEADER TIP for The Study
Because this topic can be so powerful and relevant to kids' lives, your group members may be tempted to get caught up in issues and lose sight of the deeper biblical principle found in The Point. Help your kids grasp The Point by guiding kids to focus on the biblical investigation and discussing how God's truth connects with reality in their lives.

BEFORE THE STUDY

Make one photocopy of the "Heaven's Like This" handout (pp. 55) for every four kids, and make four copies of the "Heaven Bound" handout (p. 56).

Notify kids before this meeting to bring in something important or valuable to them or something that represents something important in their lives. For example, if playing on the school basketball team is very important to them, have them bring in a basketball or a photo of the team.

THE STUDY

OPENER ▼

My Personal Heaven
(15 to 20 minutes) Have kids form groups of four. Give a pencil and one "Heaven's Like This" handout (p. 55) to each group. Say: **Read each quote about heaven, then discuss your reactions to the quotes. Give everyone in your group an opportunity to explain why he or she agrees or disagrees with each quote.**

Give kids about seven minutes to discuss the quotes. Then say: **Now you have three minutes to come up with your own quote about heaven. Work together to come up with a believable, true statement about what you think heaven will be like, and write your statement on the back of your handout.**

After three minutes, call kids back together and have them share their quotes. Then say: **Now let's see what the Bible has to say about what heaven will be like.** Assign Isaiah 65:17-25 to one-third of the groups, Revelation 7:9-11 to another third, and Revelation 21:2-7 to the final third. Have kids investigate their Scriptures, and instruct them to find what the Bible says about heaven. After three minutes, ask a student from each Scripture group to read the assigned Scripture. Then ask:

● **How would your quote or definition about heaven change now that you've heard these Scriptures?**

Then say: <u>**Heaven is real.**</u> **We don't have to worry about what we'll do in heaven or worry about being bored because we're going to be so awed by God's greatness. But God doesn't want us to think about heaven as something far away and remote—he wants it to affect our lives today.**

LEARNING GAME ▼

It's for Real!
(10 to 15 minutes) Set a stack of paper and a pile of pencils in the middle of the room. Have kids form pairs, and ask pairs to each get a pencil and eight sheets of paper. On a sheet of newsprint, write "How does its existence affect your everyday lives?" and "How does it shape your character?" Tape the sheet to the wall.

Say: **We're going to play a game of "It's for Real." I'll name some things that exist or are real. In your pairs, you need to answer two questions. First: How does its existence affect your everyday lives? Second: How does it shape your character? For example, if I say "professional sports," you might answer, "motivates me to get involved in sports" then "sports helps me strive toward excellence."**

DEPTH FINDER — UNDERSTANDING THESE KIDS

Teenage Research Unlimited, an organization that keeps tabs on teenagers' opinions and habits, has plenty of data to suggest that kids are distracted from "heavenly things." It reports that

● 69 percent of teenagers surveyed in 1993 agreed with this statement: "I always try to have as much fun as I possibly can—I don't know what the future holds and I don't care what others think."

● 35 percent of twelve- to fifteen-year-olds say success means money.

● The top five worries of kids ages twelve to fifteen are grades, looks, money, being gossiped about, and getting along with parents.

● Kids' top five attributes of a "cool" person are that they're good looking, have lots of friends, are popular with the opposite sex, are outgoing, and are funny.

● Kids say they spend a lot of time participating in these things during the week: watching TV (an average of 11.5 hours per week); listening to FM radio (10.3 hours); listening to CDs, tapes, or records (9.6 hours); hanging out with friends (8 hours); and playing sports (6.6 hours).

One of the best things you can do for these busy, distracted kids is to provide a safe place for them—a place where they can be with people who care about them, who are willing to listen to them. Only when kids feel they can trust you and open up to you about their frustrations, worries, and lives, can you help touch their lives with God's love.

LEADER TIP for The Study

Some kids may think that heaven's going to be a boring, quiet place. To help dispel this myth, take them to a sporting event—a football, basketball, baseball, or hockey game—anywhere where they'll experience screaming, passionate, and cheering fans. After the game, ask kids if they think heaven's going to be more like the game or like a quiet library. Read Revelation 4:8-11, and discuss how some of the same elements experienced at the game will take place in heaven, for example, ascribing value and honor to someone, hearing lots of noise, giving praise, celebrating, enjoying who you're with, wanting to be there, and experiencing excitement.

Quickly write your answers and initials on a sheet of paper. When you're finished writing, fold the paper into an airplane and launch the plane at me. I'll read the first answer that hits me. If neither of the people in your pair know how to make a paper airplane, switch partners with a group where both students have the skill. Are there any questions?

Say: **School is real. How does it affect your everyday lives? And how does it help shape your character? Answer the questions and make your airplanes.** Pick up the first airplane that hits you. Read the initials and read the answer. If you have time, read additional answers from the group. Do the same thing with the following words:

● Families
● TV
● Parents
● Friends
● Music
● Summer
● Heaven

Then ask:

● **Which of the things I mentioned has the biggest effect on your everyday life? Explain.**

● **Do these things affect your life in good or bad ways? Explain.**

● **Was it hard to come up with ideas for how the reality of heaven affects your everyday life? Why or why not?**

Ask a volunteer to read aloud Matthew 6:19-24. Say: **Heaven**

LEADER TIP for It's for Real

You may want to wear glasses or safety goggles to protect your eyes from being poked out by paper airplanes.

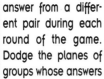
DEPTH FINDER — PROOF POSITIVE

For further study, point your kids toward these verses to discover how Jesus, the disciples, and other people attested to the reality of heaven:

● 1 Kings 8:30 (God dwells in heaven.)
● Matthew 5:12 (We have a reward awaiting us in heaven.)
● Matthew 6:9-10 (God's will is accomplished in heaven.)
● John 6:38 (Jesus came to earth from heaven.)
● John 14:2-3 (Jesus will take us back to our place in heaven.)
● 1 Peter 3:21-22 (Jesus rules over everyone and everything from heaven.)
● 2 Peter 3:13; Revelation 21:1-4 (God will bring a new heaven and a new earth.)

is real. And the reality of heaven should affect how we live our lives each day. Every action we do either stores up riches in heaven or stores riches for this earth. Since heaven is eternal, it makes much more sense to store up our treasure there instead. When we truly believe in the reality of heaven, we can live for Jesus without reservation.

CREATIVE BIBLE EXPLORATION ▼

Late Night With Bible Characters

(15 to 20 minutes) Set up the front of the room to resemble a talk show set by putting a chair behind a table and setting another chair next to the table. Have kids get into four groups, and give each group an index card, a pencil, and one "Heaven Bound" handout (p. 56). Assign one of the Bible characters to each group.

Say: **Read the Scripture verses aloud. Then discuss the questions on your section of the handout. Write your top-ten list of character qualities that your Bible character exhibits on your card. If you can't quite come up with ten qualities, that's OK. Then choose a representative who'll share your top-ten list with the group later.**

After kids finish discussing the stories and making their lists, sit in the chair behind the table and say: **Good evening, everyone. Welcome to Late Night With Bible Characters! We've compiled our top-ten lists of character qualities of a few Bible characters, and we'd like to share them with you. Our first guest is an expert on Solomon. Come on up here, have a seat, and tell me about the top-ten list you came up with for Solomon.** Have that group's representative sit in the chair by the table and read his or her group's list. Allow kids to throw the cards behind them when they're finished. Then continue, introducing the experts on Abraham, the Rich Fool, and Judas. After all the lists have been shared, ask:

● **Which characters lived as if heaven is real? not real?**

● **How did their choices shape who they were and what they became?**

● **How do you think their choices shaped their eternity?**

Say: **Faith in Jesus is all that is necessary to enter into heaven. But what we do on earth will affect our heavenly reward. It's important that we live as if <u>heaven is real</u> because we will spend eternity there. So let's take every opportunity we have to focus on what's really important.**

CLOSING ▼

What's Really Important? (5 to 10 minutes)
Have kids retrieve the items you asked them to bring before the study. Gather everyone in your church's sanctuary or to the front of your room. Put the cross on a table or the altar. Ask:

● **Why is your item important to you?**

Then say: **I'd like to tell you a little story. There was once a man who went to an auction. But it wasn't your run-of-the-mill auction. No...for sale here were unclaimed items that people, now gone, had left in safe-deposit boxes. They were precious things— photos, watches, letters, passports, and diplomas. They were so valuable to these people that they wanted them kept under lock and key. But the man wondered as he looked at all of the items years later, "How important are they to those people now?"**

Have kids put their items near the cross. Ask:

● **How did it feel to lay your item near the cross?**

● **How would it feel to let go of that thing for the rest of your life?**

● **How important will your item be in ten years? twenty years? after you die?**

● **What's truly important in life?**

DEPTH FINDER   GOING DEEPER

Biblical commentator Matthew Henry gives some background on Matthew 6:19-21: "'Where your treasure is, on earth or in heaven, there will your heart be.' The heart follows the treasure, as the needle follows the lodestone, or the sunflower the sun. Where the treasure is there the value and esteem are, there the love and affection are. Where the treasure is there our hope and trust are; there our joys and delight will be; and there our thoughts. The heart is God's due and that he may have it, our treasure must be laid up with him. Our treasure is our alms, prayers, and fastings, and the reward of them; if we have done these only to gain the applause of men, we have laid up this treasure on earth...But if we have prayed and fasted and given alms in truth and uprightness, with an eye to God, we have laid up that treasure in heaven; a book of remembrance is written there."

(Source: The Bethany Parallel Commentary on the New Testament)

Read aloud 1 Corinthians 3:10-15. Say: **Because <u>heaven is real</u>, we should be focusing on heavenly things. Not only are there rewards on earth for focusing either on heavenly or earthly things, but there are rewards in heaven.**

Give a sheet of paper and a pencil to each student and say: **Write a prayer to God, asking for help and committing to focus on heavenly things in the days and weeks ahead. Then, one at a time, come up and say or read the prayer to God. Leave your paper prayer there as a gift and commitment to God that you'll remember that <u>heaven is real.</u>**

Heaven's Like This

Read a few of these quotes about heaven taken from America Online, then discuss whether you agree or disagree with them.

● "My theory is that if there was a heaven or hell it would be really crowded so we need to take overcrowding into account. Also, practically everyone who has had a near-death experience has met relatives, so my theory needs to take that into account as well."
—PSalomon

● Well, my heaven would have harps, of course...It would have great debates, after which the participants can remain friends...We could reason and guess...use our minds. Oh...and plenty of good books!"
—MaeveMerry

● "I think heaven will be a place where we will finally be given triumph over our sinful natures, be reconciled with our new bodies, and be restored to being able to do God's will perfectly."
—XPE

● "I've often wondered about the views such as 'streets of gold' or 'mansions in the sky.' I've often tried to come up with a clear vision in my head about what heaven actually looks like and have decided on the one and only thing that counts. Heaven is being next to God and my Savior Jesus."
—Xelon

● "There's no cellulite, therefore no need for diet drinks!"
—JavaMon1

Heaven Bound

[SECTION 1]

Read the Scriptures and discuss the questions, then prepare your top-ten list.
Solomon (1 Kings 3:1-15)

1
- What did you learn about Solomon's heart or focus in his life?
- How did the attitude of his heart affect his actions?
- How would you have acted in Solomon's shoes?
- What were the consequences of focusing on heavenly things for Solomon?

Based on what you've just read and learned about Solomon, create a top-ten list of character qualities that Solomon exhibits.

[SECTION 2]

Read the Scriptures and discuss the questions, then prepare your top-ten list.
Abraham (Genesis 12:1-9)

2
- What did you learn about Abraham's heart or focus in his life?
- How did the attitude of his heart affect his actions?
- How would you have acted in Abraham's shoes?
- What were the consequences of focusing on heavenly things for Abraham?

Based on what you've just read and learned about Abraham, create a top-ten list of character qualities that Abraham exhibits.

[SECTION 3]

Read the Scriptures and discuss the questions, then prepare your top-ten list.
Parable of the Rich Fool (Luke 12:13-21)

3
- What did you learn about the man's heart or focus in his life?
- How did the attitude of his heart affect his actions?
- How would you have acted in the rich fool's shoes?
- What were the consequences of focusing on earthly things for the rich fool?

Based on what you've just read and learned about the rich fool, create a top-ten list of character qualities that the rich fool exhibits.

[SECTION 4]

Read the Scriptures and discuss the questions, then prepare your top-ten list.
Judas (Matthew 26:14-16, 47-50; 27:1-10)

4
- What did you learn about Judas' heart or focus in his life?
- How did the attitude of his heart affect his actions?
- How would you have acted in Judas' shoes?
- What were the consequences of focusing on earthly things for Judas?

Based on what you've just read and learned about Judas, create a top-ten list of character qualities that Judas exhibits.

why ▼ Active and Interactive Learning works with teenagers

Let's Start With the Big Picture

Think back to a major life lesson you've learned.
Got it? Now answer these questions:

● Did you learn your lesson from something you read?
● Did you learn it from something you heard?
● Did you learn it from something you experienced?

If you're like 99 percent of your peers, you answered "yes" only to the third question—you learned your life lesson from something you experienced.

This simple test illustrates the most convincing reason for using active and interactive learning with young people: People learn best through experience. Or to put it even more simply, people learn by doing.

Learning by doing is what active learning is all about. No more sitting quietly in chairs and listening to a speaker expound theories about God—that's passive learning. Active learning gets kids out of their chairs and into the experience of life. With active learning, kids get to *do* what they're studying. They *feel* the effects of the principles you teach. They *learn* by experiencing truth firsthand.

Active learning works because it recognizes three basic learning needs and uses them in concert to enable young people to make discoveries on their own and to find practical life applications for the truths they believe.

So what are these three basic learning needs?

1. Teenagers need action.
2. Teenagers need to think.
3. Teenagers need to talk.

Read on to find out exactly how these needs will be met by using the active and interactive learning techniques in Group's Core Belief Bible Study Series in your youth group.

1. Teenagers Need Action

Aircraft pilots know well the difference between passive and active learning. Their passive learning comes through listening to flight instructors and reading flight-instruction books. Their active learning comes through actually flying an airplane or flight simulator. Books and lectures may be helpful, but pilots really learn to fly by manipulating a plane's controls themselves.

We can help young people learn in a similar way. Though we may engage students passively in some reading and listening to teachers, their understanding and application of God's Word will really take off through simulated and real-life experiences.

Forms of active learning include simulation games; role-plays; service projects; experiments; research projects; group pantomimes; mock trials; construction projects; purposeful games; field trips; and, of course, the most powerful form of active learning—real-life experiences.

We can more fully explain active learning by exploring four of its characteristics:

● **Active learning is an adventure.** Passive learning is almost always predictable. Students sit passively while the teacher or speaker follows a planned outline or script.

In active learning, kids may learn lessons the teacher never envisioned. Because the leader trusts students to help create the learning experience, learners may venture into unforeseen discoveries. And often the teacher learns as much as the students.

● **Active learning is fun and captivating.** What are we communicating when we say, "OK, the fun's over—time to talk about God"? What's the hidden message? That joy is separate from God? And that learning is separate from joy?

What a shame.

Active learning is not joyless. One seventh-grader we interviewed clearly remembered her best Sunday school lesson: "Jesus was the light, and we went into a dark room and shut off the lights. We had a candle, and we learned that Jesus is the light and the dark can't shut off the light." That's active learning. Deena enjoyed the lesson. She had fun. And she learned.

Active learning intrigues people. Whether they find a foot-washing experience captivating or maybe a bit uncomfortable, they learn. And they learn on a level deeper than any work sheet or teacher's lecture could ever reach.

● **Active learning involves everyone.** Here the difference between passive and active learning becomes abundantly clear. It's like the difference between watching a football game on television and actually playing in the game.

The "trust walk" provides a good example of involving everyone in active learning. Half of the group members put on blindfolds; the other half serve as guides. The "blind" people trust the guides to lead them through the building or outdoors. The guides prevent the blind people from falling down stairs or tripping over rocks. Everyone needs to participate to learn the inherent lessons of trust, faith, doubt, fear, confidence, and servanthood. Passive spectators of this experience would learn little, but participants learn a great deal.

● **Active learning is focused through debriefing.** Activity simply for activity's sake doesn't usually result in good learning. Debriefing—evaluating an experience by discussing it in pairs or small groups—helps focus the experience and draw out its meaning. Debriefing helps sort and order the information students gather during the experience. It helps learners relate the recently experienced activity to their lives.

The process of debriefing is best started immediately after an experience. We use a three-step process in debriefing: reflection, interpretation, and application.

Reflection—This first step asks the students, "How did you feel?" Active-learning experiences typically evoke an emotional reaction, so it's appropriate to begin debriefing at that level.

Some people ask, "What do feelings have to do with education?" Feelings have everything to do with education. Think back again to that time in your life when you learned a big lesson. In all likelihood, strong feelings accompanied that lesson. Our emotions tend to cement things into our memories.

When you're debriefing, use open-ended questions to probe feelings. Avoid questions that can be answered with a "yes" or "no." Let your learners know that there are no wrong answers to these "feeling" questions. Everyone's feelings are valid.

Interpretation—The next step in the debriefing process asks, "What does this mean to you? How is this experience like or unlike some other aspect of your life?" Now you're asking people to identify a message or principle from the experience.

You want your learners to discover the message for themselves. So instead of telling students your answers, take the time to ask questions that encourage self-discovery. Use Scripture and discussion in pairs or small groups to explore how the actions and effects of the activity might translate to their lives.

Alert! Some of your people may interpret wonderful messages that you never intended. That's not failure! That's the Holy Spirit at work. God allows us to catch different glimpses of his kingdom even when we all look through the same glass.

Application—The final debriefing step asks, "What will you do about it?" This step moves learning into action. Your young people have shared a common experience. They've discovered a principle. Now they must create something new with what they've just experienced and interpreted. They must integrate the message into their lives.

The application stage of debriefing calls for a decision. Ask your students how they'll change, how they'll grow, what they'll do as a result of your time together.

2. Teenagers Need to Think

Today's students have been trained not to think. They aren't dumber than previous generations. We've simply conditioned them not to use their heads.

You see, we've trained our kids to respond with the simplistic answers they think the teacher wants to hear. Fill-in-the-blank student workbooks and teachers who ask dead-end questions such as "What's the capital of Delaware?" have produced kids and adults who have learned not to think.

And it doesn't just happen in junior high or high school. Our children are schooled very early not to think. Teachers attempt to help kids read with nonsensical fill-in-the-blank drills, word scrambles, and missing-letter puzzles.

Helping teenagers think requires a paradigm shift in how we teach. We need to plan for and set aside time for higher-order thinking and be willing to reduce our time spent on lower-order parroting. Group's Core Belief Bible Study Series is designed to help you do just that.

Thinking classrooms look quite different from traditional classrooms. In most church environments, the teacher does most of the talking and hopes that knowledge will transmit from his or her brain to the students'. In thinking settings, the teacher coaches students to ponder, wonder, imagine, and problem-solve.

3. Teenagers Need to Talk

Everyone knows that the person who learns the most in any class is the teacher. Explaining a concept to someone else is usually more helpful to the explainer than to the listener. So why not let the students do more teaching? That's one of the chief benefits of letting kids do the talking. This process is called interactive learning.

What is interactive learning? Interactive learning occurs when students discuss and work cooperatively in pairs or small groups.

Interactive learning encourages learners to work together. It honors the fact that students can learn from one another, not just from the teacher. Students work together in pairs or small groups to accomplish shared goals. They build together, discuss together, and present together. They teach each other and learn from one another. Success as a group is celebrated. Positive interdependence promotes individual and group learning.

Interactive learning not only helps people learn but also helps learners feel better about themselves and get along better with others. It accomplishes these things more effectively than the independent or competitive methods.

Here's a selection of interactive learning techniques that are used in Group's Core Belief Bible Study Series. With any of these models, leaders may assign students to specific partners or small groups. This will maximize cooperation and learning by preventing all the "rowdies" from linking up. And it will allow for new friendships to form outside of established cliques.

Following any period of partner or small-group work, the leader may reconvene the entire class for large-group processing. During this time the teacher may ask for reports or discoveries from individuals or teams. This technique builds in accountability for the teacherless pairs and small groups.

Pair-Share—With this technique each student turns to a partner and responds to a question or problem from the teacher or leader. Every learner responds. There are no passive observers. The teacher may then ask people to share their partners' responses.

Study Partners—Most curricula and most teachers call for Scripture passages to be read to the whole class by one person. One reads; the others doze.

Why not relinquish some teacher control and let partners read and react with each other? They'll all be involved—and will learn more.

Learning Groups—Students work together in small groups to create a model, design artwork, or study a passage or story; then they discuss what they learned through the experience. Each person in the learning group may be assigned a specific role. Here are some examples:

Reader

Recorder (makes notes of key thoughts expressed during the reading or discussion)

Checker (makes sure everyone understands and agrees with answers arrived at by the group)

Encourager (urges silent members to share their thoughts)

When everyone has a specific responsibility, knows what it is, and contributes to a small group, much is accomplished and much is learned.

Summary Partners—One student reads a paragraph, then the partner summarizes the paragraph or interprets its meaning. Partners alternate roles with each paragraph.

The paraphrasing technique also works well in discussions. Anyone who wishes to share a thought must first paraphrase what the previous person said. This sharpens listening skills and demonstrates the power of feedback communication.

Jigsaw—Each person in a small group examines a different concept, Scripture, or part of an issue. Then each teaches the others in the group. Thus, all members teach, and all must learn the others' discoveries. This technique is called a jigsaw because individuals are responsible to their group for different pieces of the puzzle.

JIGSAW EXAMPLE

Here's an example of a jigsaw.

Assign four-person teams. Have teammates each number off from one to four. Have all the Ones go to one corner of the room, all the Twos to another corner, and so on.

Tell team members they're responsible for learning information in their numbered corners and then for teaching their team members when they return to their original teams.

Give the following assignments to various groups:

Ones: Read Psalm 22. Discuss and list the prophecies made about Jesus.

Twos: Read Isaiah 52:13—53:12. Discuss and list the prophecies made

about Jesus.

Threes: Read Matthew 27:1-32. Discuss and list the things that happened to Jesus.

Fours: Read Matthew 27:33-66. Discuss and list the things that happened to Jesus.

After the corner groups meet and discuss, instruct all learners to return to their original teams and report what they've learned. Then have each team determine which prophecies about Jesus were fulfilled in the passages from Matthew.

Call on various individuals in each team to report one or two prophecies that were fulfilled.

You Can Do It Too!

All this information may sound revolutionary to you, but it's really not. God has been using active and interactive learning to teach his people for generations. Just look at Abraham and Isaac, Jacob and Esau, Moses and the Israelites, Ruth and Boaz. And then there's Jesus, who used active learning all the time!

Group's Core Belief Bible Study Series makes it easy for you to use active and interactive learning with your group. The active and interactive elements are automatically built in! Just follow the outlines, and watch as your kids grow through experience and positive interaction with others.

FOR DEEPER STUDY

For more information on incorporating active and interactive learning into your work with teenagers, check out these resources:

● *Why Nobody Learns Much of Anything at Church: And How to Fix It,* by Thom and Joani Schultz (Group Publishing) and
● *Do It! Active Learning in Youth Ministry,* by Thom and Joani Schultz (Group Publishing).

your evaluation of core belief

Bible Study Series
for junior high/middle school

the truth about
THE SPIRITUAL REALM

Group Publishing, Inc.
Attention: Core Belief Talk-Back
P.O. Box 481
Loveland, CO 80539
Fax: (970) 669-1994

Please help us continue to provide innovative and useful resources for ministry. After you've led the studies in this volume, take a moment to fill out this evaluation; then mail or fax it to us at the address above. Thanks!

● ● ● ● ● ●

1. As a whole, this book has been (circle one)

not very helpful   very helpful
1   2   3   4   5   6   7   8   9   10

2. The best things about this book:

3. How this book could be improved:

4. What I will change because of this book:

5. Would you be interested in field-testing future Core Belief Bible Studies and giving us your feedback? If so, please complete the information below:

Name _____

Street address _____

City _____ State _____ Zip _____

Daytime telephone (____) _____ Date _____

THANKS!